20 p.

THE DISTINCTIVE CHARACTERISTICS OF RE-EVALUATION COUNSELING

I have often been asked by members of lecture audiences to elucidate the differences between Re-evaluation Counseling and other approaches to human behavior. I used to try to do this, but have concluded that it was a mistake, that I will make such attempts no longer. To attempt this requires that I, in a sense, describe these other systems to the audience, and this places me in a false position since I should not really speak for these other theories. Their spokesmen and theoreticians are widely published and the questioner can easily do his own research into what each purports to offer.

I do know something about Re-evaluation Counseling, however, and, with hindsight, it seems that this is what my audiences really want to hear anyway. What are the fundamental features of the Re-evaluation Counseling system that are distinct from other approaches? After some thought, and conversations with people both inside and outside of Re-evaluation Counseling, I have assembled a list of what I think these distinctive features are. The list is still growing — perhaps the reader can point out some crucial features which I have missed. At this writing (May 1973) it numbers 35 points.

Some of these points are *unique* to Re-evaluation Counseling. As a set, they are *distinctive.*

(1) First, our definition of intelligence is basic. We define human intelligence as the ability to respond to each different situation in the environment with a fresh, new accurate response.

(2) Second, we make a sharp distinction between "feelings" and this intelligence as a guide to action. "Feelings are to be felt" is the guideline. If they are good feelings, enjoy them, but don't be guided by them. If they are bad feelings, feel them and discharge them but don't be guided by them. Logic should always be the guide. Regardless of how one feels, it should always be possible to determine the right thing to do and do it.

(3) Our concept of the basic, underlying integral nature of the human being is primarily based on the assumption of a very large amount of flexible intelligence, of the ability to come up with new, accurate, successful responses for each person with an undamaged forebrain. *The nature of the human is integral, wholesome.* The natural feeling of a human being is zest, the natural relationship with other human beings is love and cooperation. We assume this is the inherent nature. We regard distress as a disfunction rather than as a "bad side." We try to avoid the old dichotomies of yang and yin, good and evil, etc. We regard distress or poor behavior as a disfunction which occurs for definite reasons and about which something can be done.

(4) We assume that the only *source* of disfunction in a human being is an experience of *hurt,* either physical or emotional, which leaves the information input during that hurt experience in the form of a rigid, compulsive pattern of feeling and behavior rather than as useful information.

(5) We assume complete recoverability from distress, provided the forebrain is intact. This is a postulate, an assumption. None of us has completely recovered yet. The fact that it *is* a postulate has a definite influence on each counseling session. A counselor with this attitude takes very different actions than does one with different assumptions.

(6) We set a goal of total function for the human being. We reject any cultural standards of norm and assume that the human being has the capacity to flower and flourish far beyond any presently observable models. We assume that the outstanding abilities which show up in some human beings are latent in everyone, but inhibited. We set the goal of complete flowering of the human being, not simply adjusting to a particular environment or society.

(7) We assume *discharge* is the important and almost the only step in the recovery process that requires outside assistance. By discharge we mean a series of very complex processes that human beings go through that we are not in a position to define physiologically as yet. (We doubt that any physiologist is ready at present.) These processes can be observed to happen. We assume that

they are very complex, and we concentrate on what we call the dependable outward indications of these processes; tears, trembling, perspiration, laughter, angry shouting, reluctant but non-repetitive talk, eager talk, and associated with these, the process that is dependably characterized by yawns.

(8) We assume that, given attainable conditions, discharge becomes spontaneous.

(9) We understand that the precondition for successful discharge is the division of the client's free attention approximately equally between the distress on which discharge is being sought and material contradictory to the distress.

(10) The results of discharge are the dissolution of the compulsive pattern, a freeing of the frozen intelligence, and the conversion of the pattern to useful, available and evaluated information.

(11) The organization of the general techniques of Re-evaluation Counseling in a *spectrum arrangement* permits the safe, effective counseling of any individual in any state of distress. This is in practice tempered by the realization that a deeply distressed person may require enormous resource in order for a good job to be done, and so co-counselors must consider carefully their own resources of time and experience before undertaking to help a deeply distressed person. The general

rule remains for co-counselors to seek new people who will be able to co-counsel back successfully after a small preliminary investment.

(12) We assume the possibility and necessity of exhaustive discharge; that for a particular distress, every bit of stored tension can and needs to be discharged.

(13) We assume that the mind has full capacity to heal itself given the opportunity for discharge, and that ingestion of any substances other than adequate nutrition (any drugs that interfere with mental functioning — narcotics, tranquilizers, stimulants, analgesics, psychedelics, etc.) are harmful and interfere with the recovery process. The use of such drugs is incompatible with Re-evaluation Counseling.

(14) We hold to the concept that the client is in charge of the process of counseling and that the counselor is a necessary but precisely limited helper. The counselor (or the second person) is in a helping position, not in an authoritative position.

(15) Any diagnoses are made by the client, and we regard them as tentative and subject to revision after the next burst of discharge. The counselor doesn't diagnose. He will make tentative guesses in his own mind and be guided by them in his role as assistant, but will never impose them on the client.

(16) Re-evaluation Counseling is not regarded as an emergency measure to be ceased on attaining "normalcy." It is regarded as an ongoing process, as a continuing tool for living.

(17) The counselor draws no conclusions for the client. It is expected that the client will do his own thinking. The counselor is under an injunction not to let the thinking he does be communicated and get in the client's way.

(18) The client is fundamentally self-directing in the counseling process but has a "contract" with the counselor, for the counselor to intervene when the client's distress interferes with the discharge process. Experienced co-counselors are very aware of this, and beginning co-counselors operate intuitively, but this is always the basic relationship.

(19) We draw a clear distinction between the *person*, good and wholesome in every respect, and the *distress pattern*, which appears to represent the person but which is actually a foreign element, parasitic upon the person.

(20) Making this distinction between pattern and person, we are consistently *validating* towards each other and avoid the common mistake of being critical and invalidating in the name of "truth" or "sincerity."

(21) We are sure that a distinction between aware activity and unaware activity is not the same as a distinction between rational and irrational behavior. A large amount of rational think-

ing and acting takes place on an unaware level while compulsive behavior can be "faced" and not discharged and still remain irrational.

(22) The peer relationship is crucial in Re-evaluation Counseling. Co-counseling is two-way, the co-counselors taking turns. If A is client and B is counselor at this session, at the next session A is counselor and B is client. The roles are not only reversible but are regularly reversed in this main mode of Re-evaluation Counseling.

(23) We believe that theory should be in full possession of the client as far as possible. The domain of theory is not restricted to the counselor. Co-counseling works better if the client is the expert.

(24) The ongoing *counseling of the counselor* is important. No one acts as counselor without being counseled. Even a one-way client who is getting help for a fee from a professional Re-evaluation Counselor has the right to expect that next week his counselor will be in better shape than he was last week because the counselor had a session in the meantime. We determined this many years ago from experience — that no one should counsel without being counseled.

(25) The distinction we make between intermittent and chronic distress patterns is important. It took us a long time to clarify the difference between a distress pattern that is triggered now and then and one which operates all the time and encompasses the person and his behavior, and the

different approaches necessary to free the client from each.

(26) The notion of a full-time direction against a chronic pattern is crucial to success against such a pattern. The client will accept a direction contradicting a distress pattern, making it vulnerable to discharge not only in his or her counseling session but in all of his or her living. He or she will attempt to "starve the pattern to death," to deprive it of its grip on a person's life style by contradicting it and making discharge that much more available in the sessions themselves.

(27) Co-counselors apply the theory not only in sessions but as a way of life. This aspect has become prominent in the last few years. In workshops and classes where Re-evaluation Counselors meet and discuss, this engages a great deal of their attention and enthusiasm. People try to clean up their lives and live rationally by these principles. Co-counseling isn't an activity isolated from living.

In our communities we have people of all occupations. The people with common interests develop great enthusiasm for applying Re-evaluation Counseling theory in their particular fields. Classroom teachers, for example, try to change the present difficult situation in classrooms by the use of validation and support, by allowing children to discharge and setting up co-counseling relationships between them.

(28) Use of the theory becomes an ongoing project. People not only broaden use of the theory into all aspects of life, but also plan to extend its use into the future for its impact on future society.

(29) Re-evaluation Counseling spreads mostly by one-to-one communication of theory. Nearly everyone who now participates was recruited on such a one-to-one basis. (Someone experienced gave each of them a session.) A new person begins to really grasp the theory only after he or she has had his or her first session.

(30) Practice is largely communicated by "each-one-teach-one" basis. Everyone who co-counsels is encouraged to teach another individual how to co-counsel. He or she doesn't have to get permission. The teachers who teach classes and offer Re-evaluation Counseling to the public require the approval of the community, but each individual co-counselor is encouraged to teach another individual.

(31) Group and community activities grow inevitably out of the paired co-counseling relationship.

(32) Re-evaluation Counseling theory arose out of spectacularly successful *experiences* with solving peoples' problems. The successes were accidental to begin with, but they occurred. With cautious experimentation they became reproducible as the elements of the situations that had led to the first successes were located and used with other peoples' problems. As these successful experiences were more and

more dependably reproduced, the theory of Re-evaluation Counseling arose as a careful and tentative explanation of why these successes took place and what the dependable elements in the counseling situations were that consistently allowed distressed people to make such rapid gains. The successful experiences came first, and *then* the theory.

(33) The Theory of Re-evaluation Counseling grew as an *inductively logical* structure.

The mistake of attempting to explain these successes on the basis of existing confused theories was avoided by an early decision to make a completely fresh start, to include nothing in the developing theory of Re-evaluation Counseling simply because someone had said it was so or wrote a book saying it was so. We (my early associates and I) decided early in the process to be rigorous about restricting the basis of the growing theory to *our own* experiences with the clients that *we ourselves* worked with and to *only* those parts of the experiences that proved consistently reproducible.

(34) Re-evaluation Counseling has a *deductively* logical structure parallel to, and supporting the inductively logical structure which first evolved.

By the early 1960s we had accumulated a large amount of observational information from our work with clients, all of which information pointed in the same general directions. We decided at that point to attempt a deductively logical structure for the theory to complement the inductively logical structure which we had been erecting. At this point we prepared a list of 24 assumptions on which the theory was based, and published them as the Postulates of Re-evaluation Counseling. Since that time, new developments in theory have been worked out as theorems consistent with and derived from these assumptions. At the same time, these theoretical propositions continue to be checked against reality through the work of professional Re-evaluation Counselors, through the experience of the increasingly large number of co-counselors, and through the experiences of the Re-evaluation Counseling Communities.

There is a clear distinction between a conclusion reached by deductive logic, air-tight and inevitable given the starting premises, and a conclusion reached by inductive logic, by "the weight of the evidence" that is, reasoning from particular observations to a general conclusion, a process always carrying with it the possibility that one more observation could undermine the generality of the conclusion.

The greater rigor of deductive logic is illustrated by a humorous exhibit in the Seattle Science Center which illuminates this difference. It is framed from the viewpoint of the mathematician and his purely deductive logic. The exhibit goes:

THE MATHEMATICIAN LOOKS AT OTHER DISCIPLINES

When asked to prove the *false statement:* "All odd numbers are prime"

the physicist answers	Let's see . . . 3 is prime, 5 is prime, 7 is prime, 9 is . . . wait, 9 can be divided by 3 . . . but 11 is prime, and 13 is prime. Yes, all odd numbers are prime, 9 must be an experimental error.
the chemist answers	Well, 3 is odd, and it's prime . . .5 is odd, and is prime . . . 7 is odd, and it's prime . . . I guess that's enough data to say that all odd numbers are prime.
the engineer answers	All right, 3 is odd and it's prime, 5 is prime . . . 7 is prime . . . 9 is prime . . . 11 is prime . . . 13 is prime . . . .
the theologian answers	Yes, 3 is prime. Since that is so, I think we could say that all odd numbers are prime.

(35) Re-evaluation Counseling attains and requires logical consistency in its theory and practice and does not borrow from, nor hybridize with other theories and practices, even though there may be superficial similarities to them.

Today (early 1973) Re-evaluation Counseling is receiving a great deal of attention. New people are joining classes and communities at an explosive rate. Among these new participants are many professional therapists, clinical psychologists and psychiatrists who have become interested, are communicating with us and are participating in Re-evaluation Counseling. Sometimes, out of previous indoctrination, insecurity, or confusion, some new participants (professionals or laymen followers) want to mix or blend the theories and practices of other therapies and psychologies with Re-evaluation Counseling and are puzzled and offended when we firmly insist that they not do so.

(Anyone is free of course to use the *knowledge* of Re-evaluation Counseling which they have acquired in any way their responsible judgment decides, but we insist that they not *call* what they are doing Re-evaluation Counseling when they are mixing it with other practices, and that they not use such a mixture with their co-counselors in Re-evaluation Counseling Classes or in the Re-evaluation Counseling Communities.)

Sometimes people are puzzled at our objections to their mixing other theories and practices with Re-evaluation Counseling because they have experienced or read about other therapists performing some actions very similar to some things the Re-evaluation Counselor does with his or her clients and think that therefore the two sets of practices should be compatible.

What they do not realize, because in general they are not used to rigorous thinking in this area, is that the *assumptions* are different in the two cases and this being so the similarities can be ephemeral. The Re-evaluation Counselor proceeds from different assumptions and will proceed to different results than did and will the other therapist. To mix in other practices in Re-evaluation Counseling is to saddle oneself with unfaced contradictions which can lead very quickly to harmful practices which have nothing in common with Re-evaluation Counseling.

These thirty-five points characterize Re-evaluation Counseling, at least in large part. What other distinctive points about it have you noticed that I've missed?

– Harvey Jackins
May, 1973